Potty Train Simplified

Key Strategies for Potty Learning that Foster Healthy
Brain Development for Babies, Toddlers & Kids

Carl Allen

ISBN: 978-1-63750-228-0

Table of Contents

Introduction

Are you worried about potty training? Carl Allen's proven strategies for potty training toddlers will help you to get your kid out of diapers and onto the toilet.

Potty training doesn't necessarily need to be hard. This book makes it easy to get your child to start using the toilet activities fast using straight to point strategies for potty training a child, which is full of practical real-life experience and advice to take you through the process of preparing child for potty training.

. If you've ever said to yourself:

- When should I start potty training?
- How fast can I potty train my child?
- At what stage should I potty train a boy or a girl?
- How do I know if my baby is ready for potty

training?

- Why won't my child pee and poop in the potty?

- How do I avoid potty accident and failure?

- My kid was doing so well with potty but why the regression?

…and many more.

This simplified potty-training book will solve all of these (and other) common problems. This isn't theory, you're not bribing with candy, and there are no gimmicks. This is real-world, from-the-trenches potty training information needed to get done with using disposable diapers forever.

CHAPTER 1

Indicators that Your Son or Daughter is Ready for Potty Training

Firstly, you have to check if your son or daughter is preparing to be potty-trained or not. If a kid is not ready, it doesn't really matter what do, you won't be able to train them.

Here are some things to bear in mind:

1)   Is the child already in a position to stay dry for at least 2 hours or much longer throughout the day?

2)   Does your son or daughter know how to check out basic directions or do they learn how to copy you when you inform them to take action?

3) Is your son or daughter wanting to please, and do they have a need to be praised?

4) Do they now appear thinking about the potty seat, toilet or the toilet?

5) Do they now appear thinking about wearing underwear?

6) Do they now complain about diapers that are dry out or damp? Do they know the variations between the two?

7) Can they run and walk now?

8) Do they like to maintain their proper places?

9) Do they now make an effort to dress themselves?

10) Do they now let you know that they would like to pee or poop through face expressions or words?

11) Is your son or daughter now in a position to sit, and

then rise from a toilet chair?

12) Do they learn how to pull their trousers down, and put them up again?

13) Are they acquainted with toilet lingo, such as wet, dry out, pee, poop, dish, bottom level, clean, or

messy/dirty?

If your response to many of these is "yes", then it's likely that, your son or daughter is preparing to be potty-trained.

If indeed they are, check out the next section so can learn the place to start.

CHAPTER 2

Prerequisite to Potty Training

When kids learn a new skill, they rarely learn it all at one time. Typically, they process the information in manageable pieces. You have to believe and understand how your son or daughter learn to process and respond to information. The process began in the past when he was a child and learned to carry up his mind and shoulders and also to control his body. He progressed to sitting down, after that to crawling, and to walking while you hold him by hand. Shortly he was cruising the home furniture. After a period, he took those initial shaky steps, as soon as those were perfected, he began to walk. This organic sequence of occasions took from ten to twenty weeks.

Just as that you patiently and methodically helped your son

or daughter learn to do things naturally, you can motivate him to understand the countless details involved in potty training before you actively start potty training, that can do a lot of things that set your son or daughter up for catching up with the learning process when it's high time.

Ensuring Toddler's Readiness

Most kids enjoy books and like to be read to. Many great children's books, created precisely for toddlers, can be found on potty training. Make an effort to get those books which have photographs of kids with books that make use of colorful pictures of pets and likely creatures learning how exactly to use the toilet.

Reading these books before training can help your son or daughter become familiar with the theory in a fun, nonthreatening way without expectations attached. You can even make use of these same books as potty-time reading when teaching begins.

Carefully Select Your Potty Words!

Certain words are normal in particular geographic areas, plus some are more trusted than others. If you pay attention to daycare, the recreation center, or the retail shopping center, you'll soon know very well what words are normally used in town.

Here are a few of the words most used by families with small children:

Body Terms: Urination, bowel movement, vulva (everything you can see) and vagina (the canal inside), penis, buttocks/rectum, flatulence.

Family Words: Toilet, pot, potty, privy, loo pee, pee-pee, move potty, go pee-pee, tinkle, pissy, wee-wee, go wee, wee, wees, tee-tee, visit the bathroom, visit the toilet, utilize the potty, go (as in, "will you go?") poop, poopie, poo-poo, poos, caca, BM, move poo-poo, number two, utilize the potty, vulva, vagina, privates, bottom level, girl parts, penis, willy bottom level, bum, tush, toches/tucks, cheeks, fanny, behind, buns, rear gas, passing gas, passing wind, fart*, toot, breaking wind, blow off, poot, fluffer, stinker, etc. are regarded a rude term for children in a few families but regular in others.

Certain scientific or specialized terminologies sound odd when used with a kid. Can you envisage yourself asking your baby, "Have you got pressure in your rectum indicating that you need to defecate?" Instead, choose words that you'd be comfortable having your son or daughter use and understand fast. Use whatever phrases with which your loved ones is preferred and familiar; remember that these words will likely be called or used by your child in a general public place, so it is safer to adhere to socially acceptable language.

Ensure Natural Training Strategies

Babies and also toddlers accept things that happen in their diaper as normal and natural. It is not until siblings, peers, and adults instruct them there's some factor disgusting about these procedures that they think in another case. Try to let your son or daughter maintain this innocent view-point about elimination. This can help toilet teaching, and potty training becomes a more definite knowledge without any embarrassment or shame.

Don't attach negative worth to wet or messy diapers. (Ensure you avoid words like miserable, icky, stinky or smelly) Do not make a significant creation about the smell or consistency, and do your very best to caution your son or daughter's big brothers and sisters about this!

Teach Your Toddler the Language

Throughout your everyday events, coach your toddler, the phrases and meanings of toilet-related terminologies such as body parts, urination, bowel motions, and toilet duties. When enough time comes for real potty schooling, there is so very much to learn, so that it will be useful if he or she currently is more comfortable with the necessary information.

Lots of terms that are used during potty training aren't directly toilet-related but can make different concepts for your son or daughter to comprehend. Descriptive words that you'll use during the procedure are those like wet, dry, clean, flush, and toilet paper (tissue paper).

Teach your child the idea of opposites and specific purposes which will give a foundation for toilet training. Wet/dried out, on/off, messy/clean, up/down, stop/proceed, now/later, these are concepts that'll be part of the potty training routine.

It's common for parents to employ a mixture of phrases and terms during the potty process, but doing this can confuse a fresh trainee. If for instance, you question him if he would "go potty," however, the next day you asked him "to go use the toilet," and later consult him if he must "tinkle," he might not follow your school of thought. It is best if you choose your vocabulary conditions and adhere to them during the training process.

Promote Your Son or Daughter's Independence

This is the time to encourage your son or daughter to do things on her behalf, for example; putting on her socks, draw up her pants, remove her jacket, carry a plate to the desk, and climb directly into her car seat. All of these tasks nurture a sense of independence, which will be essential for potty mastery.

As your son or daughter masters each task, her degree of confidence will develop. The more she can perform, the more she'll be ready to try. Each achievement builds on previous successes, as well as your child will discover herself to be someone who can try brand new things and be proficient at performing them. This attitude will become especially helpful when it's to introduce potty training.

Make Your Child Identify the Act

Each time you change your son or daughter's diaper, you have an opportunity to train a bit about elimination. Making casual comments about elimination is an excellent method to teach. Take for instance, *"You have poopoo in your diaper."* Or, *"Your diaper is wet because you peed. Mommy pees in the potty."*

A few brief explanations as time passes are helpful. You can clarify that the wetness is pee-pee and the dark brown stuff is poopoo. Inform him or her that they are leftovers that her body doesn't need. Explain a clean, dried out diaper is a lot nicer to wear.

Help your child recognize what's taking place when you see that she's wetting or filling her diaper:

Luckily for you, if you capture her tinkling in the toilet bowl or if you feel that unexpected warmth in her diaper while carrying her. At this period you can explain what she's carrying out and let her understand that in a period like that she'll learn to perform it in the potty.

Effect of Demonstrations during Training

It can be beneficial to let your child see you or her siblings utilize the toilet. You won't need to have her view every detail; it's much enough to have her discover you take a seat on the toilet bowl while you explain what you are doing. Tell her that whenever she gets heavily pressed, she'll place her pee-pee and poo-poo in the toilet, too, rather than in her diaper.

If your son or daughter has older siblings, cousins, or friends, tell her that they used diapers when they were her age, however now they utilize the toilet. If they're available to accompany in the toilet, let your baby get a glimpse of his or her sibling or peer using the potty. Allow her understand that when she gets just a little older, she'll produce that act, too.

Don't assume all parent is ready to have little eye viewing while they utilize the toilet, and it's not essential for you to do that. If you like your privacy, after that teach your son or daughter to respect a shut bathroom and toilet door. Remember that as your son or daughter masters her very own toileting, she is more likely to stick to in your footsteps and desire her personal privacy as well. Set up the toilet so that it's safe and sound and manageable on her behalf, and keep hearing open when she actually is alone in the toilet.

CHAPTER 3

3 Days Potty Training Strategies

Now that your son or daughter is preparing to be potty-trained, why don't we talk about how exactly to do it.

Focus on a Good Attitude

A lot more than anything, you must have a good attitude. This will show your son or daughter that the experience is fun, and it's not at all something they must be frightened of. When the experience becomes fun and fascinating the procedure will be considerably more interesting.

Prepare the Equipment and Make use of a Doll!

Put the toilet chair in the toilet. It may also be helpful if you allow your child decorate the gear to increase their positive organizations with this technique.

Another technique that can lighten the feeling of this trip is utilizing a doll throughout the procedure. You are able to first suggest to them how to use the gear by using a doll. If you observe keenly, dolls often make kids feel just like they aren't alone.

By using a doll in an effort to teach a kid what they must do, they can associate easier. For instance, bring the doll to the toilet chair and allow it sit back. Make toilet noises, and then help the doll down, and say "good job" You might even supply the doll a "celebrity", or any form of praise. When the kid views this, they'll realize that "this is what I should do." They will also know that it's alright and that it ought to be done on the toilet chair. It'll obviously show to them that something good should be praised.

Where to start Potty Training

When starting off, it's best to choose an entire day when you are completely free. I know this can be problematic for some parents, but I would advise you to get the time in the event that you do, this will accelerate the training curve of the kid and make the procedure easier. In this day your son or daughter will require your undivided attention, so try your very best to ensure everything is looked after.

Tell your son or daughter something such as "Today we will figure out how to go potty like a large young man." Say this as though it's something very exciting that the kid would love. "This will be fun," would be the framework for the whole process.

For the whole first day your son or daughter will be naked or bottomless. It is because throughout the day, you are going to try to capture your child when they are peeing. You will then get them to the toilet as they are peeing. Ensure the toilet is nearby all the time and make an effort to move fast if you are getting the child to the toilet. It could be frightening for the kid if you move too fast, so ensure a satisfactory speed.

When the kid starts peeing, do not overreact. Simply inform your son or daughter in a relaxed firmness to "Keep it in," and hook them up to the toilet immediately. For males, when they may be on the toilet, hold their male organ down and train him to get this done himself. After they are done, try to reinforce this new behaviour with an incentive of praise. You can say something along the lines of "Wow, well done." We are attempting to put into action a sense of accomplishment for the kid every time this happens.

To greatly help to encourage this peeing process, also keep your son or daughter hydrated throughout the day. You should shoot for slightly more liquid than usual, but, don't overdo it.

I have to stress that it's important that you retain a strong concentration on your son or daughter during the day as you will need to catch them peeing once you can.

It is a nerve-racking time for both of you, and it helps to get some quality time with them.

Throughout the day, you may notice your son or daughter provide a funny look or behaving in a certain way before they

pee. As working out continues each day, you will observe your child begin to realize their need to pee better and better. They may be beginning to make an association in their brains between your feeling and the action of heading to the toilet.

A great deal of methods start off with you putting your child on the toilet multiple times a day.

However, I believe my way, at least for the first day, works more effectively and I've heard several people attest to this. I believe it can help the child affiliate the toilet with peeing and pooping far better.

Teaching the kid to poop

When your child is trying to poop you should notice a concentrated look, grunting or other signs of discomfort. At these times, simply sit the kid on the toilet and encourage them, inform them they can get it done. Try your very best, you shouldn't be forceful or commanding as this might make it more challenging. It is advisable to give mild encouragement and assistance. If your son or daughter begins crying, just make an effort to be supportive and try your very best to comfort them.

Praise your son or daughter if they're successful and tell them they have done well. If your son or daughter doesn't

poop or you miss them pooping on the first day, be sure to inform them "Poop goes into the toilet," in a stern enough shade that they can get the message. However, once more it is advisable to not be excessively critical of these as this is a difficult and tiresome day for both of you.

Napping

In this first day, it's important to use diapers for naps and during the night time. Naps are also very important to

keeping your child in a mood in which they will be able to

learn. It becomes extremely difficult to instruct a cranky child.

Second Day Strategy for potty Training

On day two, we will schedule toilet breaks during the day, and we remain ready to offer them help if indeed they happen beyond these scheduled times. On this day we will have the kid putting on clothes. Something important here is to make sure the pants are easy to get off. I also suggest starting the kid with heading commando for at least the next week. I believe the child is a great deal more likely to capture themselves peeing considerably faster this way. It is because it is much more of a distressing feeling for them and it is a significantly different feeling compared with putting on diapers.

Set routine each day to allow them to go directly to the

toilet. This will be ideal after meals when they are more likely to go. You may already know a time when your child regularly will do their business. If this is actually the case; then take them to the toilet and take their diaper off at the moment.

Your son or daughter's new found desire for the potty may start to waver at this time as they get more accustomed to it. It's important to keep your son or daughter amused at this time, so be sure you bring a toy or a publication to the toilet with them.

If you are just starting, don't worry if indeed they haven't pooped by the end of your scheduled program. What to do is to simply put their diaper back again on. That is an extremely different environment to allow them to poop and may take some time to allow them to get accustomed to it. Just keep on as typical before next planned practice.

Third Day Strategy for Potty Training

It could be easy to get frustrated if your son or daughter is progressing slower than you hoped. You must remember every child is different and placing pressure on them will only inhibit their learning. Every child learns at different rates We should keep our persistence.

On day 3 and beyond, we are heading to continue as before with our scheduled times throughout the day.

Now we will attempt to market our child to let you know if indeed they need to go. Do that by emphasizing how well they are doing. We are satisfying them with praise to help these instructions and training create the contacts they need in their brains. If this doesn't happen immediately, don't feel bad; your child will eventually reach the stage of letting you know.

Teach the kid how to completely clean up

A large part of toilet training a kid is supporting them in understanding how to completely clean up too, especially with girls. What you want to do is tell her that she should carefully wipe herself from the front (vulva area) completely to the back (anus area) and not otherwise, so that bacteria wouldn't normally fester her body. Teach her so she'll know what's hygienic and what isn't.

Once they learn how to clean themselves, then train the kid how to flush their waste. Suggest to them how it's done in the toilet and bathroom. Once they understand how to do it, they will be more accountable as it pertains to cleaning up.

Obviously, don't forget to inform the child to clean his/her hands afterward. Again, proper cleanliness is vital.

Some Rewards and Incentives During Training

Provide them with a book or a toy

It will be quite helpful if you give your son or daughter a toy or a potty-training related publication for kids (Once Upon a Toilet, I'D LIKE My Toilet, Sam's Toilet) so that toilet training is a fun and engaging learning experience for him.

At first, you have to remain with your son or daughter while they're at their toilet place, just to ensure that they're using the potty chair properly, and that they are not uncomfortable. Eventually, they'll figure out how to tell you firmly to stay away, and they know what must be achieved already. For the beginning, however, it is important that you stick with them initially for proper support. If you continue vacation, it's important to bring the toilet chair or check if the area has a child-friendly bathroom seat, and that means you can continue practicing. It's important to be constant at this stage in your son or daughter's life.

Other Incentives

Here's a set of other bonuses which you can use:

1. Colour Books. Help the child become more creative by allowing them work on a colour book after every potty work out. Let them choose the reserve they would like to use so that they will be interested.

2. Buy a Drink-and-Wet Doll! You may think it's icky, but what better way to teach a child how to potty than to buy her a fresh toy; by utilizing a doll, especially the Drink-and- Damp Doll. What this doll will do is that you will get to give food to it or allow it drink, and then she pees after. Bring her to the toilet seat as well as your child and he/she will surely realize what must be done and also have fun at it, too.

3. Help them decorate a Door Hanger. Colour it, add stickers, let them write, etc. What matters is that they can have something to hold on the entrance when they feel like they need to go toilet. Once they have something like this, they will be more than willing to toilet because they are going to be thrilled to use what they had made earlier.

4. Make a Lollipop Tree. That is only a makeshift tree created from lollipops. Give one to your child after each

toilet program and chances are, they will look ahead to those classes more.

5. Make a Happy Jar. On popsicle sticks, reveal fun actions you can take per day, or maybe through the weekend. For instance, see Frozen again, visit a theme recreation area, make pizza, etc. Put them in a big glass jar and also have your child pick one after every potty program. Surprises often make kids happy, and this one will surely help him learn and be happy at the same time.

6. A Toy "Vending" Machine. Buy one of those toy vending machines that have little playthings included, and let your son or daughter get one after every potty session.

7. Make an even jar. Put some labels beyond your jar. The

main one on the cheapest would be for the first couple of days of toilet training, and the main one on the top would be the best reward. Let your son or daughter add two marbles after each successful toilet training program, and they'll be interested in learning because they'll recognize that in a few weeks' time, they'll get something excellent. When you yourself have the right bonuses, toilet training would be so far better.

How to approach 'NO'

Eventually, you might be met with a solid "no" when you ask your child to visit the potty. It's important you don't get this to a battle of wills. This will be counterproductive, instead, respect their decision.

Don't get upset if indeed they then have a major accident, simply reinforce that they are going to the toilet to pee. If indeed they do, it is important you don't comfort them and inform them it is fine. In case you do this once they have experienced an incident , this could reinforce the behavior as your child doesn't understand the subtleties of vocabulary yet.

Resistance should come eventually so expect it and arrange for it. If you don't make a huge deal from it, their level of resistance should be temporary.

Chapter 4

How exactly to Keep your Toilet Training Methods Working

Obviously, when you toilet-train a kid, you do not just stop when you are feeling like they've discovered everything. There are certain things you should do to ensure that the skill becomes internalized.

Think about it this way: suppose you were trained a lesson on a totally new subject today, would it not just be there in your brain right away? Probably not, you would most certainly have to revise the information once or twice before it sank in.

So, as it pertains to toilet training, you have to ensure that you do as follows:

Be Patient, even when the kid says THEY DON'T REALLY want to visit Potty

Well, maybe he just will not want to look yet. Or possibly, he's timid or doesn't know very well what to do.

Yes, this is frustrating, especially because you understand you're just wanting to do the right thing. But, you might just terrify or traumatize the child if you go and get mad at them because they do not want to go to the toilet.

Have a Laidback Approach

Again, your son or daughter will learn better when they feel just like toilet training is a great experience and that it is not something they must be scared of. When you feel so angry and strict, it's likely that, your son or daughter will feel just like toilet training is scary or they are being reprimanded, that isn't the type of thing you want to foster. The key here's to realize a child learns via positive reinforcement than when they feel reprimanded.

Clap your hands, Laugh and Keep a lively Atmosphere during each Program

You must understand that kids are naturally playful. Even if it requires them a few attempts to make it happen. You have to understand that they're attempting and that alone is already a very important thing.

The very second your child gets on the potty seat, go forward and praise them. This is already an accomplishment. When the child feels that they're being motivated early on they become more confident about themselves. Be the type of mother or father who's willing to business lead and encourage him every step of the way.

Pulls-Ups or Underwear

This is dependent on the child or however, you should address this issue according to your child's Personality and their experience with toilet training.

For example, if certain children are used to diapers, they could be inclined to remain and keep playing after incidents happen. Whereas other children have a feeling of self-pride when each goes to the toilet so when they feel a major accident coming, they'll hurry to the toilet. I really do not recommend permitting them to wear diapers through the first few days of training. It is because it will require the child's drive to get to the potty.

It is also useful to test your child in different conditions as they might be toilet trained at home, but when you take them to other places, this may be completely different.

So, it is an activity of learning from your errors from this stage. If possible, prepare for the most severe, I would recommend using diapers for a little while after your son or daughter has been trained, particularly if you go out. If you want to introduce underwear to a child who is toilet trained but put off by the inconvenience of going potty, I would suggest switching to underwear. It'll become unpleasant for the kid, and they'll act out necessarily. You can even add in a supplementary inspiration, by getting special underwear to them, for example, a set with superheroes to them or a common T.V show personality.

Cost is also one factor as draw ups could be more expensive than regular diapers and are also preferably an extremely temporary solution.

Potty Training Your kid away from Home

If you are on vacation, it's important to bring the toilet chair or check if the area has a child-friendly toilet seat, which means you can continue practicing. It's important to be constant at this stage in your son or daughter's life. Understand that they can not learn everything immediately. Again, things such as this always require devoting some time. They don't really just happen right from the start. Keep in mind that just because you've taught your child how to be potty-trained today doesn't mean they'll already be an expert by tomorrow. They could need to relearn lessons. So that it is best never to get upset, and also to simply suggest to them the procedure again if they're confused.

Respect YOUR SON OR DAUGHTER'S Learning Curve

Children have different learning curves. Some learn easily, but others simply don't, but that will not mean they're not perfect or there's something amiss or terrible with them. Albert Einstein didn't speak until he was four years of age, people learn at different rates, and we shouldn't judge.

When you start comparing your child with others, you're also beginning to start a painful relationship between you two. Cut it out, be patient, and know that your child will learn eventually. Put yourself in their shoes and figure out how to keep an eye on this stage in his/her life.

Be Consistent

Consistency is the main element to the success of almost anything. If you wish to train your son or daughter, know that you need to be consistent. Get it done on plan, and it's likely that, they'll pick and choose it up faster than you think. Once you retain this at heart, you'll make things easier for you both.

Be sure to Go Toilet Fast

Now, when you see indicators that your son or daughter wants to visit the toilet or use the bathroom, even whether it's not on the timetable, go and bring them to their toilet place immediately. Take note that if indeed they wish to urinate or toilet, which is out of routine, you don't need to get mad or scold them. Actually, you should go forward and praise them because they're informing you or displaying to you that they want to urinate or toilet, that is already a noticable difference on its own, rather than them using diapers on a regular basis.

At night, it might be better to bring them to their toilet place or potty chair prior to going to sleep so bedwetting could be avoided particularly if they're already putting on underpants. If indeed they want to pee during the night, inform them to wake you up and please show patience to help them out.

Chapter 5

How to know if Your Kid is Potty-Trained Effectively

So, how exactly would you know that your child is already potty-trained? Here's what you have to be mindful of:

They know, plus they let you know if their underwear is wet: A major sign a child has already been potty-trained or is there is if indeed they know they have wet their underwear. That is an indicator that they are already hygienic, plus they know that they need to go someplace to pee or poop, and not only in their underwear.

They're wanting to get their rewards

Why? Because they know that what they're doing is

something good, plus they want to show they are learning. When a child learns the ideas of rewards and positive reinforcement, they start to have that healthy competitive streak in them. This is something good because it shows that they're understanding what you're attempting to instruct them. They know they'll get rewards if indeed they take good action, so of course, they'll focus on doing that.

Each goes to the potty chair and try particularly when they feel just like they would like to pee or poop. Another big sign that they are learning is when each goes to their seat, and make an effort to go to the toilet. For just one, they want to please you, and they also know that is right. So when they make an effort to do what's right, this means they are learning, and you're doing something right.

They're pleased with their new underpants

If they want to choose new underpants, this means that they understands they're no more an infant and because they are no more a "baby," they'll be more responsible about their pee and poop!

Chapter 6

Symptoms a Potty-Trainee (Child) must See a Medical Doctor

There's an occasion when your child appears to have an exceptionally hard moment getting potty-trained because it's an indicator that they probably have to be seen by a health care provider.

How will you know if your son or daughter needs to see a doctor? Keep these exact things at heart:

They strain while trying to pee

This is an indicator that there surely is something wrong. Usually do not await it to worsen because even though you can't see anything, there could be something amiss, so take him to the physician right away.

They haven't had a BOWEL MOTION in Three days

A person, especially a child has to have a bowel motion every day. Normally, there might be a blockage in the rectum, and it could bring infections, and these are things you do not want your son or daughter to be suffering from. It might simply be because he ate something that has made it hard for him/her to poop. In any event, Medical assistance should be sought to be sure.

They're still bedwetting, and they are already 5 years of age

That is a problem that some parents encounter with their kids. Actually, around 90% of kids damp the bed, but the problem gets worse if the kid is already 5 years and above. Sometimes, bedwetting is inherited. But other times, certain issues make bedwetting happen, some of these are the following:

1. Deep Sleeping: Some kids are deep sleepers and battle to awaken to pee.

2. Low Anti-Diuretic Hormone: When a child is afflicted with this, his hormones automatically tell his kidneys that he shouldn't urinate a lot, or that the kidneys shouldn't make a lot of urine. Therefore, what goes on is that a child produces the hormones when he's asleep-and thus, bedwetting happens.

3. Delayed Bladder maturation: Some kids' bladders do not mature as fast as others and their bladder does not talk to their brains while they're asleep.

4. Constipation: Sometimes, a youngster wets the bed because he's constipated.

5. Small "Practical" Bladder. Sometimes, a kid's bladder

sends indicators to the mind that it's already full even if it is not and so, bedwetting happens.

They have frequent stains on the underwear

These might be poop that got away when it wasn't time. Sometimes, it's not merely bowel staining you have to keep an eye on them generally, blood loss or indications of wounds or laceration. Usually do not hesitate to consider taking him to the physician right away.

They've learnt how to use the potty, but nonetheless have wet pants occasionally

This happens. Sometimes, a child is already trained, but there are occasions when he gets too moist maybe because he has bedwetting or shame issues, and such issue needs to be discussed before they worsen.

He only pees every 8 to 9 hours

Even for an adult, this is not healthy. A normal person should pee every 3 to 4 hours. In any other case, the bladder might suffer, particularly if the individual has a naturally small bladder. Whenever a child will not pee just as much as he should, it can result in issues with his kidneys. So, make sure you have him checked immediately.

Their Pee Hurts or Burns or They Have Intermittent Pee Stream

These are symptoms that a person has Urinary Tract Infecton, and that's not an easy thing to cope with. Sometimes, it causes the genitals to blow up, or the child to suffer from rashes, and of course, humiliation, sooner or later.

They Complain of Hurtful Bowel Motions

Periodically they could have problems with bowel motions

that are really hurtful because the bowel can't escape the rectum easily, or because there are irritations and blood loss involved. Understand that some kids can't easily speak up with what they're feeling and it's your task as a mother or father or a guardian to make sure they feel comfortable conveying what they feel to you. Don't allow things get to the point of being worsened before taking them to be observed by a Doctor.

CHAPTER 7

Advance Potty Training Strategies

Once you've decided about how you'll approach potty training with your kid and gathered all of your supplies, it's nearly time to start the process actively. Following are a few points to consider as you progress.

Keep in mind the two miracle factors; the teacher's excellent attitude and kind patience will set the pace for the toilet or potty-training journey. Take a breath, relax, and appreciate the knowledge with your baby.

Have a Realistic Expectations

Understanding how to master toileting is normally a huge

task for just a little child (kids). Mastery comes into play with time and patience. Sometimes will be more effective in some children than others. Sometimes when the house is tranquil and the day to day routine is definitely in place, your son or daughter will significantly have more success.

Less Clothing Strategy

If you're fortunate to begin training in warm weather, or when you can turn heat up in your house during training, hold your toddler in only training pants for a week roughly. Children often resist coping with ON/OFF requirement during teaching, since it takes so very much time and effort based on their limited skills. Therefore, the less clothing to cope with, the better!

Some parents let their children roam naked during training, but it isn't for everyone. Consider it before you bring in the theory to your baby, because he or she is more likely to like the freedom and could surprise you by carrying out a bit more of it than you expect. You might want to consider your family's method of nudity. How are things managed during bath time? How can you respond if your son or daughter walks in when you are dressing? If your family culture is certainly one of modesty and you suddenly let your son or daughter roam the home naked, it could send him or her some complicated mixed messages.

However, some families are even more relaxed about your body's natural state. Kids, siblings, and parents bathe jointly, toddlers play in the toilet as Mommy showers and dresses, and little males potty trained while peeing alongside Daddy. If this describes your family style, then you might look for a small extra time to help your child tune in with her body's elimination process.

One of the various other things to take into account here is that whenever using the naked strategy, all those early mishaps (among several others) will be unhindered by clothes and property unprotected wherever your son or daughter might be, and it will not be his or her fault or whatever you can prevent. For those who have carpeting or home furniture that may be ruined by accidents, you may take working out of the backyard or choose to go the almost naked approach instead and pop a set of training jeans on your little one.

Make the Potty Child-Friendly

Can your child easily open the door and turn on the light? Reach the toilet paper? Get right up to the sink? If he or she is facing difficulty addressing and using her potty, she'll be less thinking about using it routinely. Also, if she counts on you to perform everything on her behalf, you'll be passing up on a wonderful facet of potty teaching: encouraging your son or daughter's independence is vital.

Many small children are suspicious of empty rooms, and several fear the dark. There is nothing scarier compared to the cavern of a dark toilet. Through the training months, and perhaps actually for an extended period after schooling, accept that you'll either need to accompany your kid each time or keep the way and toilet carefully well to chase apart any unwanted shadows.

Take It Slowly

If you feel relaxed about the procedure, it's likely your son or daughter will as well. Ironically, the much less you push, the quicker the outcomes will occur.

The more you hurry, the much longer it will require. Even if a day time or an additional deadline looms, don't hurry the process with an excessive amount of strength and pressure. Being even more relaxed can help your child find out more conveniently and will get this to be less demanding for you too.

Training Pants or Disposables (Diapers)?

Once your child gets a general idea and has started having daily success on the potty, you might want to change from diapers or disposable pull-up to cloth teaching pants to make things go along even faster.

The drawback to thickly padded disposable diapers or super-absorbent training pants is that they disguise wetness so very much that your son or daughter probably isn't bothered about it, whereas cotton training pants, or disposables with a stay-wet liner, signal wetness immediately and aren't extremely comfortable to wear when wet or messy. This can help your child to be more alert to what's happening down there.

Also, be sure you keep your son or daughter's pants a little loose so your baby can pull them easily. Training slacks or pull-ups ought to be a size larger than necessary. You desire them to be manageable for your son or daughter, without being so big that they droop.

Naps and Bedtime

Many children will remain in nighttime diapers for a year or much longer after daytime achievement. Nighttime dryness is attained only once a child's biology facilitates this, you can't hurry it, so don't also try. (Occasional bed-wetting is known as normal until approaching age six.)

Maintain a routine of placing diapers or disposable pull-up on your kid for naps or bedtime. The moment he or she is awake, remove it and also have him or her utilize the potty because so many children will eliminate soon after getting up. Switch your son or daughter out of night time diapers when the morning hours diaper is regularly dry.

Dress Him or Her for Training Success

It's more challenging for a toddler to get to the toilet in time but having the complication of snaps, zippers, and buttons. Many a trainee managed to get to the toilet and then have a major accident standing before the toilet, wanting to undress. For another couple of months and probably actually longer, your son or daughter should, whenever possible, avoid wearing pants with buttons, snaps, belts, or zippers and T-shirts that hang beneath the waist. Be sure that your son or daughter can remove her clothes easily and quickly. Regarding dresses, get them short more than enough to be able to remove them completely and well taken care of.

The very best clothing for a fresh potty trainee is a T-shirt and shorts or slacks with an elastic waistband. Make certain these are relatively loose fit so that your son or daughter can easily have them up and down.

At the start of training, you might want to have your son or daughter actually remove his or her trousers and underwear when he or she uses the potty, because there are a great number of new things to consider and having a wad of jeans around his or her ankles could be distracting and partially lowered slacks can become splattered. If you do not have him remove his trousers, feel absolve to help him consider his clothing off and place them back on, also if he can perform it himself. Needing to dress and undress in about ten situations a day will work fast for a dynamic toddler and may result in disinterest in using the potty at all. Don't worry, though he or she will adapt to this section of the process very quickly.

Potty Training Abroad/Far from Home

New trainees could just be getting more comfortable with the potty routine in the home but are unlikely to really have the same success in public areas or while traveling from one place to another. It could be irritating for a mother or father to have to handle repeated incidents in the automobile or while abroad or away from home. There are numerous methods to handle being abroad with a kid in training.

You can simply opt to keep your son or daughter in diapers or disposable pants when abroad. Most children very easily adjust to the idea that there exists a change into diapers or pull-ups when you go out. Create a schedule: the kid goes potty and places on pull-ups before you go out and then adjusting back to training trousers or underwear when you come back home.

Other options listed below are to put your son or daughter's diaper or pull-ups more than his training jeans or make use of a waterproof diaper cover more than his training slacks. He may experience been happier if he will keep his big boy trousers on, yet he'll experience the wetness if he comes with an accident. It's sort of a mid-step that may keep you calm in the automobile while helping him discover that he or she is growing up.

If you'd prefer never to put your son or daughter on diapers when you are away your home, ensure that you are ready to handle on-the-street potty phone calls and potty mishaps. Bring along a portable potty for use in the automobile and a folding chair adapter for use in toilets. Cover the automobile seat with plastic material, and for cleanup, provide along wet wipes, plastic material luggage, and paper towels. Prepare yourself with a complete change of clothing, and perhaps socks and shoes.

And be sure you bring your persistence and good humor, as well. You will have bad incidents, therefore accept them, clean them up, change your son or daughter's clothes, and move on.

CHAPTER 8

Behaviours During Potty Training

Firstly, I have to cover some ground on the subject of boundaries and limits; after that, I'll hit particular behaviors I've seen in potty schooling. Boundaries and limitations have a poor rap in parenting lately. They can appear mean or draconian or too authoritarian. Many parents don't have confidence in any consequence or discipline. I want to state outright: *I do not advocate, nor do I believe in hitting or beating a kid ever.*

This is most likely the trickiest issue addressed in this book separating out behavioral conduct from potty training. There exists a lot for your son or daughter to understand when potty teaching your children. Certainly, the first couple of days, and maybe actually the first couple of weeks, are filled with learning. Learning, naturally, requires making some errors and/or having some incidents. However, there exists a difference between learning and behavior or habit. When your kid is showing behavior, and after all of the poor variety, the behavior must be addressed.

You are potty training around two-year age range, and around the same time, you might see various other two-year-old behavior. This might well be the first time you are seeing your child act, but it's normal. The awful twos aren't only a cliché; they are real. Throughout normal development, your son or daughter must test limitations. It's his work. He needs to find out where the fence is, as they say. The reason your wall in your backyard is there is indeed not to make your child wander and get misplaced.

Limits and boundaries will be the fence in your child's psyche. With them intact, just while in your backyard, your child feels safe and sound, knowing where he may go and may not go.

A trend in contemporary parenting is to assume that the kid is with the capacity of deciding good stuff for himself without having to be provided any boundaries or limits. That is not the case. I frequently look to the Montessori system for how exactly to allow children to make some decisions while also providing boundaries. Within a framework, the kids are absolved from making choices; however they are not free to carry out whatever it is they need.

The children all consume lunch collectively. You can't make a couple of kids get a snack in the fridge and leave this up to them to choose if they are hungry, it could lead to mayhem. The kids all go outside jointly, whether one is tired or not really. Our children need some fences. Within those fences, we can enable tremendous freedom.

What I see, both from my experience and in my work is that most of us parents have a problem with providing freedom within boundaries. In our quest to improve free-thinking, kids are not offered enough framework to allow them to feel safe.

I see kids raised with no limitations or boundaries who by enough time they are age five or six, are wild and incredibly hard to control. By this, after exhibiting out-of-control behavior, not that they must be "controllable" just like a puppet.

Imagine the stress your child would feel if you were driving, been at the backseat, and he or she has zero idea of where you were heading. I've extrapolated that idea even more. Imagine if your son or daughter were responsible for providing you the directions, and which you followed their instructions. Proceed left. Go right. No. Stop. Wow. You'd quickly be lost, yes? That's where points will get mucky with the oft-touted child-led style of parenting. You could be child-led for the reason that you pay attention to and validate your son or daughter's opinion, but you just can't follow your child's lead through life. Both of you will get dropped. *The automobile you are driving is usually life, and it's your task to learn where you are going.* Ironically, most of the parents I've known in my own personal life are striving to give the youngster a "freedom" childhood. Still, how free is your son or daughter if he's entirely responsible for the direction the automobile is traveling. It's hugely anxiety-provoking. A free childhood ought to be about chocolate or vanilla, and something else.

All this is especially true in case you have a spirited or strong-willed child. I frequently work with parents who have a kid fitting this explanation. This child is generally demanding and will be challenging with regards to potty training as well. Still, this child requires boundaries and limits just as much as, or even more than, your garden-variety child.

All well and great, but what does this need to do with potty training?

Well, occasionally behavior kicks up during potty teaching. And because potty schooling is so wrought with emotion, it becomes hard to draw it aside from behavior. I also discover that parents will endure all types of behavior during potty schooling that they wouldn't work in other circumstances.

For example, one of the primary challenges parents today encounter during potty training gets their child to take a seat on the potty. Yes, you can go through to them or sing to them. I state it's alright to play with a mobile device seeing that as a distraction in the beginning. But, when you inquire your son or daughter to sit to go potty, your son or daughter should sit. Today, to a lot of individuals that sounds severe.

You show your son or daughter to sit and they don't. *How can you handle that?*

I'm requesting because-whatever your response is, that's how you're likely to handle it during potty training. When it's supper, it's time to sit and consume. When it's potty period, it's time to take a seat on the potty.

Once you encounter behavior during potty training, do

your very best to put it right into a different context. That will assist you to figure out how better to deal with it in the context of potty schooling. It's your parenting duty. I do not really nor have I ever comfy telling people the way to handle behavior generally. That's why I'm providing you a framework to work with, and you may make your own parenting decisions.

Many parents say, "We don't feel safe making him sit." I agree. I don't believe you should force your son or daughter to sit. Nevertheless, it's worth pondering precisely how fearful we are because of the potty. Many parents dread doing anything unfavorable around potty training. Utilizing a firm or stern voice seems contrary to these parents, and they're worried about traumatizing the kid. This is where another scenario will come in handy. Everyone has held their kid down and strapped them in the car seat. Even though they are kicking, screaming, and hitting. We perform it because we should go somewhere, and we need them to be safe. Has your son or daughter ever been traumatized by that rather than wished to sit in the automobile front seat someday? I'm guessing No. Again, I'm not saying you should exert pressure on your child onto the potty or strap him down, or anything remotely like this. I'm simply pointing out that fear of traumatizing a kid by conveying the message that you mean business has gotten a bit out of control.

Another thing to bear in mind may be the difference between *"the kid you have" and "the kid you want."* You have a child you have, definitely not the kid you need. This is also true during potty training.

I can give you recommendations about any special conditions you might have, but we can not change your zebra's stripes. Still, that is hard for all of us to admit and hard to keep in mind. Most of us want the well-behaved,

loving, courteous kid. We got what we want. Still, our choice is fierce. When you are potty training, take care not to linger in the property of "I want him . . ." We can deal with what we have, but we can not cope with fantasy.

There's another aspect to "a child you have." If your son or daughter shows a particular "problem"- say he's whiny, or she's resistant or susceptible to histrionics and tantrums, you will have this same kid if you are potty teaching. No judgment; there is absolutely no behavior I've not really seen. Still, I discover parents who in some way think potty training will happen in a bubble-that the rest of the behavior the kid exhibits is somehow not likely to appear even though it's potty training. That is a big transition, so these behaviors can not only be right there, but they may get magnified for a brief period. Again, it's all great. Just keep your anticipations level as well as your love big.

Whatever your child's personality is, I can't change that or correct it; that's built-in the child's physiology. If your son or daughter is exhibiting the behavior you do not like, or you are feeling is usually disrespectful, you will likely see that same behavior during potty schooling. What I could tell you is how exactly to deal with a few of the behaviors you find in potty training.

Here's a clear exemplary case of behavior. Say your son or daughter did ideal for a couple of days. Suddenly, she doesn't want to utilize the potty anymore. This may appear to be a defiant "NO!" or it could seem she just can't be bothered with this. If she sat and peed/pooped on the potty several time, then we realize she can perform it, it's that easy. If she subsequently chooses never to, it's behavior.

In case you are feeling unfortunate or just a little heartbroken that it isn't heading as you intended, it's likely that your son or daughter needs more learning. If you feel as if you are being pranked, if you feel anger, or if you feel like strangling your kid, I'll wager it's behavior. Usually, parents have a pervasive sense when they are coping with behavior but don't carry out anything because they're terrified of "traumatizing" the kid.

Having boundaries and pursuing through won't traumatize your kid in any sense. When you have a youngster who you understand is taking part in you, the very best move to make is provide a small, instant, appropriate consequence. For example, take away the play toy he was using when he wet his slacks, or consider restraining him from the activity where he was involved.

Toddlers don't have that extended way of thinking. For this reason, sticker charts are ineffective. Toddlers don't have the thought process to state, "Wow. I've six stickers; yet another and I'll have a week of staying dry out!"

The small, immediate consequence can be helpful when you aren't sure whether he needs more learning or is exhibiting the behavior. I believe I've managed to get clear that satisfaction and self-mastery ought to be the motivation behind potty training a child effectively. However, for a few children that by no means clicks in, plus they need some exterior motivation to nudge things along. Some parents react such as, "But I'll feel terrible if I provide him a consequence, and he needs even more learning." Removing a little toy consequently won't scar your child forever. And it's the quickest way to get a remedy. If your child can't utilize the potty realizing that his toy is sure to get placed on the fridge for one hour if he doesn't, you can wager that so far he needs more to learn, and he won't be scared. If your child can do it all, you then know the incidents are because of behavior. I'm talking about real-world potty training, not theory. Effects are sure to get you your solution the fastest.

Some parents say, "Isn't a consequence only the opposite of an incentive? I'd rather give incentive for the behavior I want rather than provide a consequence for what We don't want." I am aware of the idea behind this and, yes, generally, positive reinforcement is most effective with children. Nevertheless, we get back to that notion of expected behavior. The problem with benefits and potty schooling is that they get sticky. The stakes must be continuously raised to ensure they work. If you are likely to reward for peeing, where else can that lead? I'd rather curb undesired behavior than prize the hell out of excellent behavior. Else, you finish up with a youngster who expects to end up being rewarded for everything.

I fully have confidence in benefits for exemplary behavior, and I also think that bad behavior gets a consequence.

CHAPTER 9

How to Solve Toilet Training Problems

If you have been thoughtful, patient and organized, toilet training may still not go according to strategy. There are plenty of typical complications that appear during the schooling process. The most typical problems are teaching resistance, excessive incidents, refusal to have a bowel motion on the potty, constipation etc. The very best spot to start is usually to contemplate the many usual known reasons for toilet teaching complications and find if you cannot figure out the reason for the issue. This chapter provides specific suggestions and solutions for the issues that these circumstances cause through the potty training process.

The first rung on the ladder to solving any issue is to have a deep breath and do it again after me (using the power of confessions): *"My kid will figure out how to make use of the toilet. They all do. This as well shall move."* More than 98 percent of children grasp daytime toileting by age four, and with persistence and the proper plan of actions, your child are certain to get there, too.

The Most Commonly Known Reasons for Toilet Training Problems

- The child isn't ready (lacks the correct physical skills).

- The child isn't ready (emotionally, socially, or behaviorally).

- The child doesn't know very well what he or she's

supposed to do (communication).

- The child is becoming too distracted with something else to value going potty.

- The kid is uninterested in training.

- The child can be fearful of, or unpleasant with, some aspect of training.

- Existence of a power struggle between your child and the parent.

- There's too much tension and pressure surrounding the process.

- The mother or father has unrealistic expectations.

- The parent isn't carrying out a toilet training program; it's hit or miss.

- The parent isn't ready (lacks time, endurance, or desire to carry out an idea).

- The mother or father and caregiver don't

acknowledge an idea and are sending mixed messages.

- The mother or father is confusing normal mishaps with failure.

- The routine doesn't match the child's elimination pattern.

- The strategy used doesn't match the child's learning style or personality.

- The strategy used doesn't fit the parent's personality or teaching design.

- There exists a physical or medical deterrent (such as constipation, disease, or uncontrolled allergies).

Another important idea to understand is that you could lead a kid to the potty, nevertheless, you can't help to make him or her fill it. That is your child's undertaking, not really yours. You can teach her, you can prepare the required tools, and you will maintain positivity and supportive, but maybe for the very first time in her youthful life, the greatest result is completely in her power.

Potty training appears like a huge little bit of chocolate cake. With a part of ice cream. Sprinkled with chocolates! Maybe even more amazing.

Endeavor to examine the prior list of commonly known reasons for toilet teaching problems and make an effort to figure out which part of it are obtainable in the form of effective toileting mastery for your son or daughter. After you have a deal with one of those fundamental reasons, it'll open up your brain to all types of new solutions. Afterward, read over the topics that adhere to that match your problems.

Excessive Accidents

It's common for kids to have accidents if they are not accustomed to using the potty bowl. But if incidents don't gradually fade out as time passes, or if your son or daughter is having more experience moving in her slacks down in her potty, it may seem training is certainly going nowhere. Following certainly below are a few comments and recommendations.

"He comes with an accident each day!"

If your son or daughter is not used to potty training, it really is flawlessly normal for him to have a number of accidents each and every moment of commencement of training. Even kids who've been trained for half a year or even more may have a major accident once a week. The very best solution is usually to be ready for these with appropriate cleaning materials, quick access to a change of clothing, and a calm attitude.

One approach that will help reduce the amount of accidents is that you should become familiar with your son or daughter's signals of impending desire to visit the toilet and take your son or daughter to the potty when you suspect he or she must go. Do not request if he must go, because he'll most likely say no. Rather, invite him to check out by saying, *"Let's go potty."* Or provide a choice, saying, *"Do you wish to make use of your potty or the big toilet?"* Or just hold him by the hands and lead him to the toilet, saying, *"Come with me, kiddo."*

There's one very last thing to consider.

Do you provide your son or daughter more attention (great or poor) when he comes with an incident than when he provides achievement?

Turn the tables. Tidy up mishaps quickly and without emotion, and offer lots of compliment, hugs, and interest for each productive potty visit.

"She never helps it be released into the toilet. It usually goes into her pants."

Your child might not be hearing her body when it tells her it is time to go. Or she gets so occupied with her play that she attempts to yank it apart, or she thinks she can take it a lot longer than she can really.

You may consider moving the potty nearer to her and

which makes it easier on her behalf to go. Create a potty nook near her play region and maintain her dressed in very easy clothes. Once she gets utilized to heading when she must, you can move the potty seat back again to the toilet.

You may try having a potty party weekend. Don't announce this to your child, just make an idea in your own brain. Stay house all weekend and go out in the same space as your baby. Provide plenty of salty snack foods and a lot to drink. Check her for signals and lead her to the potty once you think she might need to proceed, plus execute a potty operation every hour roughly. Give stickers, little prizes, or treats (think about her preferred salty chips?) to maintain her motivated and interested. The hidden benefit to this strategy is that you could like a weekend of one-on-one quality time together with your precious little kid.

Constipation and Refusal to have a Bowel Movement on the Potty

One of the most common and frustrating toilet training roadblocks is whenever a kid is unwilling to pee on the potty but needs a diaper, or uses his slacks, for bowel motions. Some children will in actuality hold their bowel motions and create serious constipation, which additional complicates the issue.

Children typically resist bowl movement on the toilet, or restrain from going, for just one of these reasons:

- Bowel motions take too long to hold back, and a dynamic child dislikes needing to take a seat on the potty for a protracted length of time.

- After being accustomed to the squashed feeling of

stool coming out right into a diaper, the sensation of allowing it to loose in to the air is normally unsettling and strange.

- A child is accustomed to standing or shifting during a bowel motion and sitting even on the potty can be an uncomfortable change of schedule.

- Your son or daughter thinks the stool is usually part of his being and doesn't realize why he ought to flush it away.

- A poor experience, such as ending up being splashed on the bottom level with urine or water during elimination or having a messy incident, causes a child to avoid having it happen again.

- Discomfort from a previously hard or hard stool makes a kid afraid to poop on the potty.

- A current case of constipation which is stopping

usual elimination.

Don't try to resolve the problem without understanding why it exists. Once you determine your son or daughter's impetus for staying away from bowel motions, you can generate the perfect strategy to help him or her have a natural elimination process.

Potty Training Resistance

You thought your son or daughter was ready. You believed you were ready. But things aren't going according to strategy. Following are some typically common mother or father statements with challenges and solutions.

"He Won't Even Try!"

If your child appears totally clueless, he probably is. For his lifetime he's peed and pooped in his diaper rather than also noticed this elimination. Right now you want him never to only notice but keep it and then place it some-where else! It is time to go through potty books, have a sibling, friend, or parent demonstrate; provide a few step-by-step lessons; and maybe have even some bare naked playtime to greatly help him observe and experience what's happening straight down there.

It's possible that your son or daughter offers to try but feels more overwhelmed. He might have had high anticipations for himself and feels he's failed. He might just need help knowing that this is not a one-day work but will need him quite a long time to learn. Compliment him for the things he can do, regardless of how little, and build on those.

I'd also recommend that you retake the readiness quiz by accessing several readiness quiz freely available online and ponder on each issue, rather than tagging down the solution that you desire to be right, indicate what's actually true. Your son or daughter might not be prepared just yet. And in the event that you currently know that, but nonetheless you need to continue potty schooling, refill your basket of tolerance, place a smile on your own face, and grab the fanciest methods in this book.

"She's tantrums when I make her take a seat on the potty."

If your son or daughter views sitting down on the toilet as a punishment, it's likely there's been an excessive amount of stress or pressure on her. If things are actually awful, you may need to stop teaching for a week or two to provide you both a breather. However, for those who have made some progress, you might not want to stop what you've achieved. Rather, make potty period more pleasurable. Add books, play toys, music, storytelling, or singing to your toilet training strategy. Begin the fun before she actually sits straight down by having a parade of elimination into the toilet. Virtually all kids thrive with a parent's lighthearted one-on-one playtime, so concentrate on this aspect for some time, without challenging a deposit each time she uses the potty.

When you are feeling your baby is enjoying potty visits, then start to take her in a regular schedule of each one and half to two hours or whenever she appears like she must go. When she starts to be successful, then compliment her and offer her with a sticker or prize. Quickly she'll dominate and end up being independent.

"I've tried everything in the book."

What may be the issue! Your poor small pottier is indeed confused he doesn't understand which end is certainly up! Have a step back and refine your program. Don't allow it to get complicated. Go over the potty-training guidelines to assist you clarify your potty schooling plan to ensure that it really is simple and clear.

Chapter 10

Myth of Toilet Training

Finally, below are a few common Toilet Training Myths-all debunked for you!

MYTH 1

"EASILY put my baby on the toilet chair when he's 1 to at least 1½ years of age, he'll easily know what's going on!"

Your child will most likely not know the actual potty he's to begin off with, and never mind how to utilize it.

You are to guide him. Help him know very well what the toilet seat is. Follow the tips that were pointed out earlier. Be the guiding pressure that your son or daughter needs you to be. Do not expect your child to understand what something is about when you have not shown them yet. Everything begins with you.

MYTH 2

"Your son or daughter's life will be ruined if you screw up his plan for toilet training."

No. You are not heading towards ruining your son or daughter's life because you have smudged his toilet training schedule, or allowed him to visit the potty if it is close to his bedtime.

Potty training, just as much as it is perfect for your child, is an excellent training for you, too. It teaches and shows you patience. It also allows you to have confidence in what your son or daughter can do, rather than what he/she cannot do. Toilet training differs for everyone, and you won't clutter up your child's life if you fall into errors. Learn from the mistake, and don't address it as something awful.

MYTH 3

"It'll lead to quarrels between my child and I."

Never think of potty training this way. Instead, think of it as a way to help you and your child's relationship which is important for his growing years. Think about it as an effort to show your son or daughter that you care genuinely. Additionally, it is a period where you can spend quality time with them. Understand that you are helping your son or daughter grow into the best person he/she can ever be.

Just like other things in life, when you concentrate on the positive part of toilet training, you will realize how amazing it is. You will always remember this particular period throughout their life, and even though it might be demanding now, you would cherish the remembrance later in life.

Conclusion

Many thanks once again for purchasing this book. I am of high hopes that it would enable you to know how you can teach your child as well as how to get it done well!

The next thing is to ensure that you follow the tips given in this book so that you can potty train your child well. Be proud of your child's eagerness to learn, and his every achievement, and you will both prosper.

Finally, if you enjoyed this book or if it is helpful in one way or the other, then let me ask you for a favor, Would you be kind enough to leave a good review on this book page? It would be greatly valued!

Dedication

I dedicate this book to all parents who want a successful
and happy child with toilet training.

www.ingramcontent.com/pod-product-compliance
Lightning Source LLC
Chambersburg PA
CBHW071722210326
41597CB00017B/2559